Lizzie's L

Written by Edwin Johns
Illustrated by Kelvin Hawley

Lizzie and her grandmother
were in the backyard.
Grandma was digging in her garden,
and Lizzie was kneeling on the grass.

"Look, Grandma," Lizzie said.
"I found a lizard. It's so cute, isn't it?"

Lizzie wanted to touch the lizard.

Grandma said, "You'll be careful with it, won't you? Don't grab it by the tail."

"Why not?" Lizzie asked.

"Its tail could break off," Grandma said.

"I can keep it, can't I?" Lizzie asked.

"You can keep it for a little while, Lizzie.
Then you have to let it go. You won't hurt it,
will you?" Grandma asked.

"No, Grandma, I'll be careful," Lizzie answered.

Lizzie gently picked up the lizard.
Her grandmother was emptying their lunchbox.

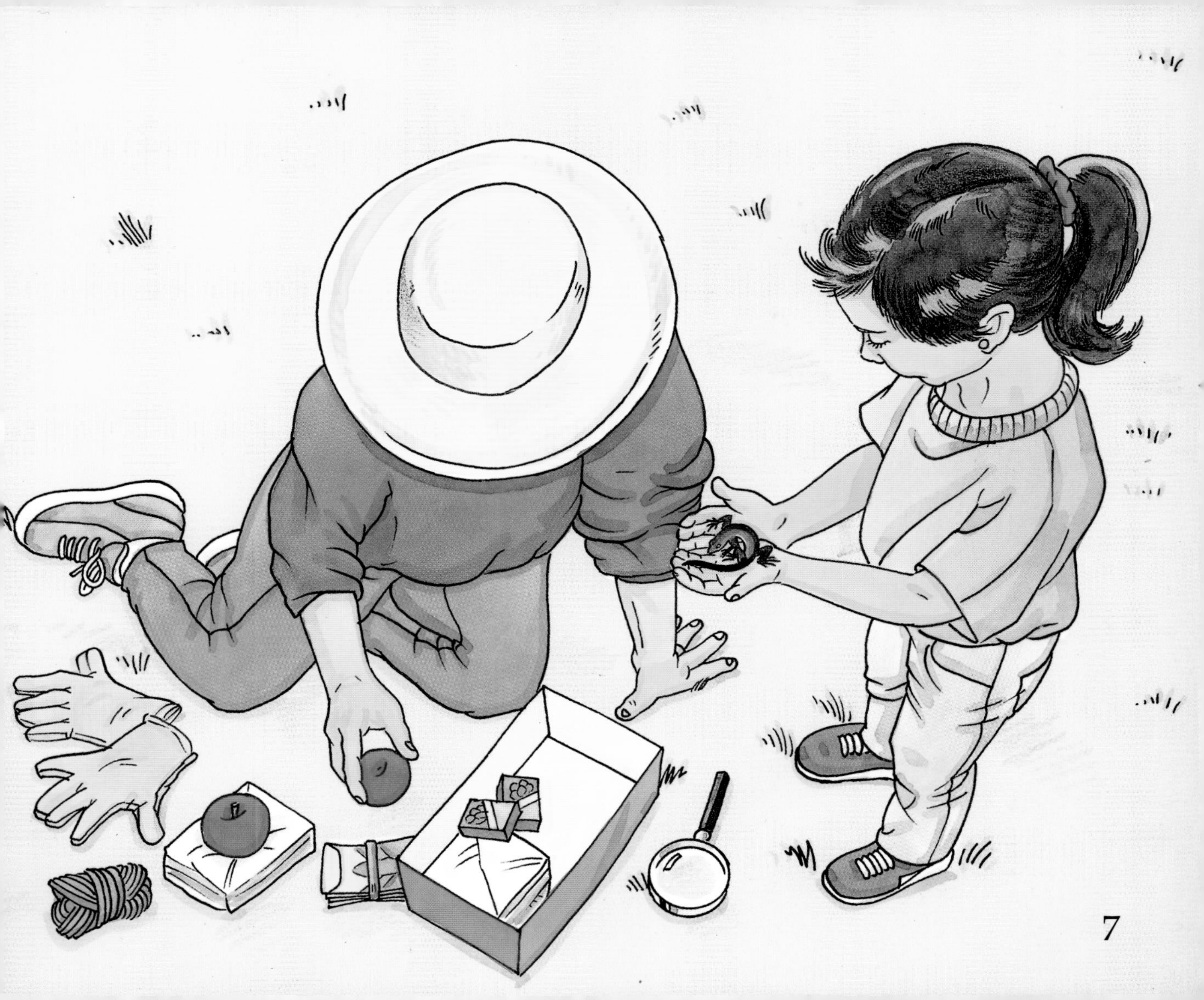

Lizzie carefully put the lizard into the box.
She put some rocks and soil in the box, too.

The lizard was sitting on a rock
and looking at Lizzie.

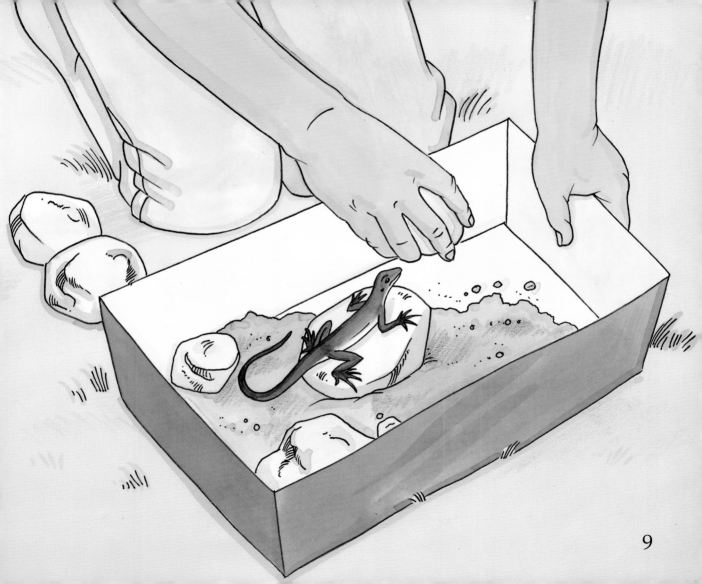

"Grandma, look! It's blinking," Lizzie said.

"Look carefully. A lizard has two eyelids on each eye," Grandma told her.

AN EYELID
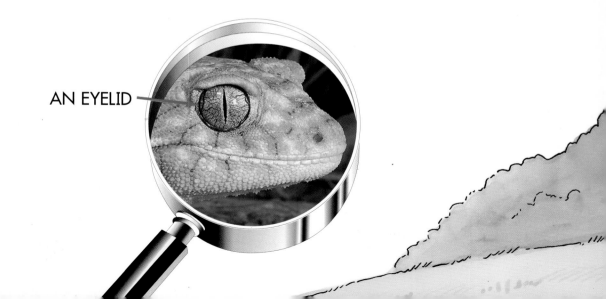

10

11

Lizzie was looking at the lizard through a magnifying glass.

"It doesn't have ears, does it?" she asked.

"Yes, it does!" Grandma said.
"It has a small ear opening on each side of its head."

"Then it can hear me, can't it?" Lizzie asked.

"Yes, it can, Lizzie," Grandma answered.

AN EAR OPENING

AN EAR OPENING

13

"What does it eat?" Lizzie asked.

"It eats small insects, like flies,"
Grandma said. "Lizards don't chase insects.
They wait quietly and let the insects
come close. Then they catch them."

Lizzie touched the lizard gently.

"It feels cold, doesn't it?" Grandma asked.

"Yes," Lizzie answered. "Why is that?"

"It's a reptile," Grandma told her.
"So it's cold-blooded. Its body temperature
changes with the temperature of the air around it."

Lizzie was looking at the lizard
through the magnifying glass again.

"It has scaly skin, like a snake," she said.

Grandma said, "That's right.
Look at the pattern of the scales."

SCALES

Then Lizzie took the lizard out of the box
and let it go in the garden.

"Can we find out more about lizards?" she asked.

"Sure!" Grandma said. "Let's go inside. We can use
the computer to look up lizards on the Internet."

21

Lizzie found lots of information.

Lizards have been on Earth
for millions of years.
They live almost everywhere
in the world.

Some lizards are very large,
and some are very small.
Some use tricks to protect themselves.

- Some can change their color
  to match the colors around them.
- Some can make themselves look scary.